a little book on soul care

Paul Francis

To Glenwood Church

Thank you for the journey.
(And what a journey it's been!)

Commendations

I believe that this little book can make a *big* difference in our lives.

Rob Parsons, author and speaker

I am attracted to anything that addresses the care of the soul. The Church tends to be drawn to power and leadership themes, building numerous ideas about the successful Christian life. But nothing works without having a healthy soul. No leader lasts, no church has solid foundations, and no ministry is powerful without the ongoing restoration of one's soul. I love this book! It's easy, it's practical, and it's positive both for those who are just beginning to think about how to shape their life and for those who need to know about making the soul their priority. Wherever you are in life right now, you'll find this wonderfully encouraging!

Christy Wimber, pastor, teacher and author

As a church leader, evangelist and creative thinker of many years standing, Paul Francis has a big passion for those on the fringes of faith. People who want to grow in their spiritual journey but don't find it easy or straightforward are the people his heart beats for – and it's a good thing it does. Too many church leaders are so busy singling out their high-flyers that they hardly notice the not-quite-sures lurking in the margins. Born from the experience of helping many such people find their way, this little book is a winsome and engaging introduction to a sustainable spirituality. For those taking their first steps in faith it will be a highly valuable resource. For those who have been so long on the journey that it has become complex and cluttered, it might just serve as the beginning of a thorough detox. This is a breath of fresh air. I recommend it for you – but I also bet you know at least five people you can give it to!

Gerard Kelly, Co-Director of the Bless Network

Acknowledgements

This book has come from the years I have spent walking with Jesus and journeying with many people. Each one of those people has had an impact on my life, so they have contributed to the book in no small way – although they don't know it! Thank you all.

I'm especially thankful to Care for the Family for their belief that this book was worth printing. In particular, I would also like to thank June Way, Sheron Rice, Alicea O'Connor, Caroline Adams and Hugh Griffiths who helped edit and refine the book to make it a much better read. They had lots of patience!

Rob Parsons is a great friend who has given me help, wisdom and support over many years. He is one of the people who helped me through my darkest moments.

I would also like to thank Woodlands Church, Bristol for the use of some of their material used in Chapter Four.

Finally, I would like to thank the leaders of Glenwood Church – Norman Adams, Rachel Treseder, Nkini Pulei, David Rees, Jane Francis and John Gallacher. Thank you so much for your wonderful support and encouragement.

Contents

A message from Paul

The car needs an MOT – you take it to a garage.
You are not feeling well – you go to the doctor.
You have an exam to take – you plan out a timetable of revision.
You are going on holiday – you make sure you have the directions.

Your soul is downcast – where do you go?
Your soul needs refreshment – where do you go?
You're feeling emotionally drained – where do you go?

Just before I turned 40, I burnt out. I crashed and went into a deep black hole. I was diagnosed as suffering from acute anxiety and depression. I took anti-depressants and was off work for almost six months, but it took me another two years to get back to a place where I felt I was 'me'. Since that time, I have walked with an emotional 'limp', a weakness, and I take more care of myself. Much of what I write about in this book is shaped by this life-changing time.

But as I came out of that period of depression, I realised that not only was I washed out and burnt up but my spiritual tank was empty. And this scared me. I didn't want it to happen again.

This little book is about some simple principles that I have learned that have helped me maintain my emotional and spiritual well-being. I hope it will help you.

Paul

Foundations

1

Who am I?

How you start off in life will often determine your destination.

So, if you grow up believing that you are:
  useless
  worthless
  a mistake
then the chances are that you're going to have a low opinion of yourself.

This belief is what many people live with. It frames their whole life.

For centuries, people have often believed that even the Church's message to them is that they are worthless, wretched and abominations! And so they live their lives with little hope and belief in themselves.

But how they see themselves is not the reality. Sure, there are times when we all feel wretched and that's a hard place to be in, but it's not the truth about us. My hope is that this small book will help us deal with those feelings of worthlessness.

Because that is not how God sees us.

In the beginning God created the universe, day and night, land and seas, mountains and valleys, trees and plants, animals and fish, and after each one was created He looked at it and said:

"It is good."

He then created humanity and looked at it. He did not say, "It is good." He said:

"It is very good!"

When God created the earth He was pleased with it all, but with human beings, He was very pleased!

In the Psalms, we discover some of the most wonderful poetry ever written, and in one of them, David writes this:

"I praise you because I am fearfully and wonderfully made" (Psalm 139:14).

God created us in His image and gave us value, dignity, love, freedom and choice. However, after the story of creation in the book of Genesis there is the story of how humanity made a seriously bad choice. It resulted in giving us a flaw – a bias. It is something inside us that at times distorts who we are.

So if you were to ask me for my view of humanity, this is what I'd say:

"We are fearfully and wonderfully made, but we have a serious flaw."

That is a good place to begin a journey. And if we begin it here, we will arrive at a different destination altogether.

A better one.

A more fulfilling one.

One that liberates us to be the people who God created us to be.

I don't deserve a soul,
yet I still have one.
I know because it hurts.

Douglas Coupland

The importance of the soul

Douglas Coupland, author of *Generation X*, a title that gave a name to a new generation, has many great quotes. This is one I love:

"I don't deserve a soul, yet I still have one. I know because it hurts."

People may not have a word for it, but all of us know we have a soul.

It's the part of us that makes us feel alive.

It's the part of us that connects us to one another in a deep and meaningful way.

It's the part of us that watches a glorious sunset in amazement and feels something inside us that simply goes, "Wow!"

It's the part of us that aches and longs for something more.

It's the part of us that feels downcast.

It's the part of us that can be bruised.

It's the part of us that can be so thirsty that no amount of water can satisfy it.

In Genesis it says that when God created humanity, He breathed life into them. The word breathe in Hebrew is *Ruach* (which can also mean spirit). God breathed His breath, His Spirit, into us and created *Nephesh*, a word that means living creature or soul. It is this that makes us different to any other created thing.

It is the part of us that cries out for God.

It is our soul.

Dallas Willard has written many books related to the theme of soul care and describes the human dimensions that work together to make us who we are. These include:

The will. This is one of our greatest gifts as it is where our ability to choose is located. Our will is not what makes us a person, but clearly, it is very important!

The mind. In the ancient world, the mind was regarded as the centre of our thoughts and emotions. These flow through us all the time in habitual patterns. Unhealthy thought patterns damage us, so an important part of maintaining our spiritual health is to develop healthy thought patterns.

The body. Our body has been described as our 'little kingdom'. It where our will has an opportunity to be in charge – where it can exercise discipline and control.

The soul. According to Willard, the soul is the part of us that seeks harmony, connection and integration between our will, mind and body. It is the 'deepest' part of us and is what separates us from the rest of creation. In the Bible, the word soul could be interchanged with the word person. Your soul is what integrates your will (your intentions), your mind (your thoughts and feelings, your values and conscience), and your body (your face, body language, and actions) into a single life.

So a healthy soul is one that is ordered – where there is harmony between the will, the mind and the body.

An unhealthy soul is one that experiences disintegration – and sin always causes disintegration.

Jesus said, "What good is it for someone to gain the whole world, yet forfeit their soul?" (Mark 8:36). For many years I thought Jesus was referring to the afterlife and what will happen to us if we give ourselves to the 'world' and ignore our soul. But I now realise that Jesus was referring to this life.

If we pay attention only to our mind, will and body – ignoring the spiritual side of our lives – our soul will begin to wither and ultimately 'die'.

Soul care is very important if we truly want to be alive.

It is essential because it is an essential part of life!

Spirituality is not an option
we choose or reject ...

... to be human
is to be spiritual!

The monk and the snowman – authentic spirituality

A few years ago, my wife, Jane, and I were in France. We went to an exhibition of photographs and it was one with a difference. The photos were of monasteries from around the world and the photographer had taken them all from a hot-air balloon. There were some great shots, but about a third of the way around we came across one that made me laugh out loud.

It is of a monastery in Northern Italy and it's obviously winter as the ground is covered in snow. In the middle of a large quadrangle, there was a big white blob, which I realised was a snowman. A black squiggly line led up to it showing where someone had rolled a ball of snow to make him.

I just loved the thought that somewhere in Italy there is a monk who makes snowmen.

If I'm honest, that's not what I normally imagine when I think of a monk!

But I also laughed because that monk is me! When it snows I, too, love to make snowmen.

The problem was that I'd grown up in a Christian culture that clearly taught that having fun was not part of the spirituality of a leader.

But after a long journey, I have learned that it really is part of my spirituality.

All that I am is spiritual – including the desire to make snowmen! We need to be the people God created us to be, and knowing that has freed me up.

Being spiritual is not simply about Bible reading, meditations and prayers.

Certainly they play a very big part, but simply to be human is to be spiritual – and to be spiritual is to be human.

Laughing, crying, having fun, suffering, eating, praying, reading and walking are all part of us being spiritual.

Life in rhythm

Are you tired? Worn out? Burned out on religion? Come to me. Get away with me and you'll recover your life. I'll show you how to take a real rest. Walk with me and work with me — watch how I do it. Learn the unforced rhythms of grace. I won't lay anything heavy or ill-fitting on you. Keep company with me and you'll learn to live freely and lightly.

Matthew 11:28, The Message

Balance

All of us lead busy lives, and it is increasingly difficult for us to carve out any time outside of work and home responsibilities. How do we find a balance that works for us in all that we do?

A good friend of mine is a psychologist and informs me that for life to work we need to keep four things in balance.

Work   Not necessarily paid – it could be taking care of the children, elderly parents, voluntary service.

Leisure   Doing things you enjoy – reading, mountain biking, walking, watching films.

Social   Meeting friends, doing good things in community.

Spiritual Soul care.

There are 168 hours in a week.

Of those, an average of
40 are given to work and
49 are given to sleep.

What do we do with the rest?

A useful exercise I've done to try and gauge whether those things are in balance in my life is to take five minutes to answer the following questions (honestly!):

There are 168 hours in a week. How much time in an average week do you give to:

- Family, friends, spouse, children?

- Work?

- Leisure and social activities?

- Soul care?

So how did you do?

If you are anything like me, the answers are a bit scary!

Now let me ask you another question ...

When life gets tough, which of those things are the first you stop doing?

Over the years, I've noticed that when I'm under pressure it is spiritual and leisure activities that I stop doing first. When stressed, everything in me goes into active mode.

As soon as I'm awake, I just want to get going and sort out whatever the problem is.

After spiritual life and leisure activities, the next thing to go is my social life, and so I have less time for my wife or friends.

Work? Well, that can't stop as it defines who I am!

In my experience, this process becomes a spiralling vortex which, if not stopped, will suck the life out of me, so that in the end I will die.

I won't die physically (though tragically this can happen to people), but I will die to who I am and what God has called me to do.

So how do we keep a delicate balance between these four parts of our life?

One word ...
... rhythm.

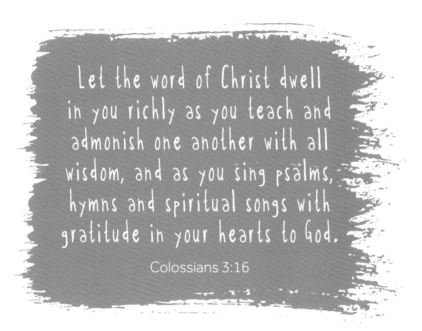

Let the word of Christ dwell in you richly as you teach and admonish one another with all wisdom, and as you sing psalms, hymns and spiritual songs with gratitude in your hearts to God.

Colossians 3:16

Finding your spiritual rhythm

When I first became a follower of Jesus, I discovered that a lot of Christians talked about the need to have a 'quiet time'. As I was a teenager, this seemed a very odd concept – a quiet time! Did it mean I should just be silent for a given amount of time? And what should I do in the silence? Daydream? Think about rugby? (I loved it!) At the age of 16, a quiet time was definitely not something that appealed to me.

Back then a quiet time meant having a disciplined time, each day, which you spent reading and studying the Bible and then saying your prayers. These in themselves were not the problem: they are excellent things to do and are essential to the well-being of our soul.

The real issue was that the faith culture of the day was based very much on fear and religiosity. As such, I did these quiet times primarily because I wanted to say I had 'done' them and could feel proud of myself.

I did not do them out of a desire to spend time with my Father.

It wasn't until I went through my time of burnout that my view about quiet times changed. As I began to get better, I realised that my spiritual tank was empty.

If I was to fill it back up again, I recognised that I had to change a number of things about my lifestyle.

I had to find a rhythm of life that allowed me to spend time with, and develop my relationship with God. I needed to take care of my soul, body, heart and mind.

All of us are so wonderfully and fearfully made – each of us unique. Therefore, the rhythm we develop is also unique to our personality – your rhythm will be different to mine.

Some of us are extroverts, others introvert.

Some of us are visual learners, others are word learners.

Some of us learn from touch, others from movement.

If you are someone who loves reading and can devour books, deciding to make reading the Bible part of your spiritual rhythm is no big ask.

However, if you struggle with books and the thought of having to read something fills you with fear, simply *reading* the Bible as part of your spiritual rhythm may not work as well as it might.

But *listening* to an audio version of the Bible or meeting up with someone who will read it with you – that might be very different for you.

We all have the potential to find a spiritual rhythm that works for us.

The thorny issue of time and guilt

We know we should spend time with God, but life is crazy.

Say you have two children. The youngest wakes at 5.30 am and you just about get them sorted out and back to sleep when big sister wakes up. It's not even 7.00 am! Then you have to get them ready and off to school and nursery so you can get to work for 9.00 am. After work, there's dinner, bath time, bedtime stories and just enough time to sort the dishes and washing up. You then collapse into bed and before your head hits the pillow, you're fast asleep.

Or what if you've just left university and started your first job. You're at the bottom of the career ladder and need to put in the hours to make your mark. By the time you leave the office, you're almost too tired to bother to get a meal.

I can hear your heartfelt cry: "I have no time, and you going on about finding a rhythm does not help me! On top of that, you're making me feel guilty that I'm failing God in some way."

This is partly what this book is about. First, to let you know that you are not failing — in fact, you're doing remarkably well just surviving!

It's not about trying to carve a rigid time slot in to your day, as I did in my early days as a Christian.

This is different. I'm talking about finding a rhythm for your day that works for you.

It could be as simple as taking five minutes as you are driving to and from work to talk and listen to God instead of listening to the radio, or putting a sermon on your iPod when you go for a walk.

That's it!

Rest

When God had finished His creation He did something which seems very alien to us in the Western world – He rested!

The Bible tells us that making Adam and Eve was the final part of God's creation and He did that on the 'sixth day'.

The next day, the seventh, God rested.

So Adam and Eve's first experience of life was rest!

God rested.

Adam and Eve rested.

Rest is part of our DNA.

So why do we struggle so much with the concept of rest? After all, God means it for good.

To remember
the Sabbath is
to rest, to pause,
to catch one's breath.

At the height of Communist Russia, an edict was sent out that all workers needed to work seven days a week in serving the State. This began to happen, but what quickly became evident was that far from increasing productivity, it lessened it! Furthermore, the number of people taking time off because they were ill increased.

The human body is not designed to work seven days a week. We are not designed to work 60 hours a week. If we maintain this sort of lifestyle then our body begins to break down, our relationships suffer and our enjoyment in life diminishes.

Part of our rhythm of life is to rest.

To remember the Sabbath is to rest, to pause, to catch one's breath.

So take a day of rest!

How to incorporate rest into your daily rhythm:

- Take 10 minutes for silence at lunch three times a week.

- Last thing at night, as you lie in bed, go over the day and give God thanks for the good stuff that happened. If you can't think of anything good that happened, then simply thank God that you got to the end of another day.

- If you do not have one, find a mentor/spiritual companion and spend some down time with them.

Self-care is never a selfish act – it is simply good stewardship of the one thing I have, the gift I was put on earth to offer others. Anytime we can listen to true self and give it the care it requires, we do it not only for ourselves, but for many others whose lives we touch.

Parker Palmer

Small hinge, big door

Part of the secret of finding a rhythm that works for us is to recognise that it may well only take a small change to our lifestyle to make a significant difference.

I recently heard a friend of mine, Paul Gutteridge, make a simple but very helpful point: it only takes a small hinge to open and close a very large door.

We may feel small and insignificant – that what we do does not contribute to anything.

The reality is rather different. In the great scheme of things, what we think is inconsequential could really be a small hinge that will allow something so much bigger to happen.

Spiritual rhythms are a bit like the small hinge. While we may only give five, ten or thirty minutes a day to our time with God, the effect on our lives, church, communities and work is so very big.

The sacred space

3

Creating a sacred space

The original New Testament was written in Greek, which is a very descriptive language. When it comes to talking about one of the rhythms of life that Jesus practised, it uses the word *eremos*. This can mean 'desolate place', 'wilderness', 'wasteland' and 'abandoned place' and it's the word that is also used to describe the places where Jesus retreated to pray.

While I did not realise this at the age of 16, space to be quiet is an essential part of spiritual rhythm. If Jesus sought the *eremos* place then surely each of us needs to find the modern equivalent.

When we bought our first house, it had an outside toilet! My father was thrilled as it took him back to his childhood – memories of running out to it in the dark of the night, the cold, the fear of rats, and the newspaper used as toilet paper! I really could not understand these fond recollections! We used our outside toilet as a storage space.

About 16 years ago, I came home to discover that the roof and part of the wall of the outside toilet had collapsed! It needed to be knocked down and re-built.

This was around the same time that I was beginning to learn about daily spiritual rhythms and the need for a 'sacred space'. This is a space you create to spend time with God and it can be anywhere.

For me, I decided it needed to be a room, and it was to be the old toilet! My father was mortified!

But I was determined to make it happen, ploughed on, and turned it into a 1.5 metre square prayer room.

This has become a sanctuary for me. It is the place I go to meet with God.

There's nothing special about the room as you can meet God anywhere. But I thought about the idea when I came across a phrase that was used by monks in the old Celtic tradition:

"Go to your cell and the cell will teach you everything."

This advice was given by the abbot to a young monk who came to him and asked for help with a problem he was facing. In a monastery, each monk has a small room, known as a cell, which is simply furnished with a bed, desk, chair and a cross on the wall.

Telling the monk to go to his cell was to tell him to go back and spend time with God.

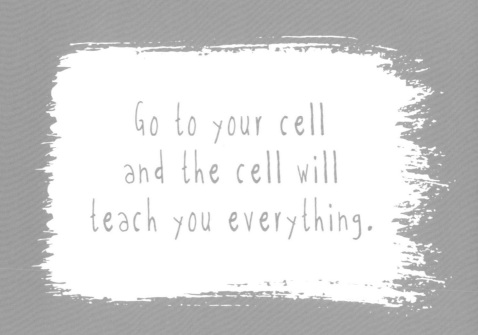

Go to your cell
and the cell will
teach you everything.

Not many of us will have the privilege of a small room, but the room is not the issue. It's finding a place where you can be still and be with God. This could be:

- A particular chair in a room.

- The kitchen sink – use the time you are sorting the dishes as your 'cell'.

- Driving to work – this could be the only 20 minutes during the day when you are by yourself.

- A walk in the park.

I'm sure you get the point!

Go to your cell! Go find your *eremos*!

Love the Lord
your God
with all your heart
and with all your soul
and with all your strength.

Mark 12:30

For us to maintain a spiritual rhythm we need practices that are realistic, achievable and sustainable. What follows are some practical suggestions based on what has helped me find my rhythm. My hope is that they will help you to do that also.

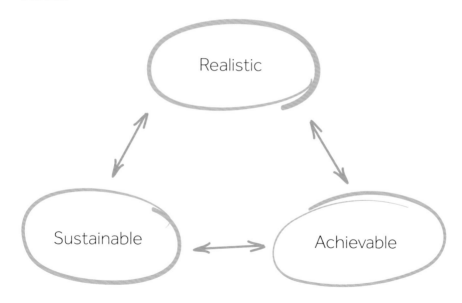

Understanding prayer – the chair

I was speaking at a young emerging leaders' conference and during the break, a student asked me a question: "I'm new to all this as I haven't been a Christian for very long. Can you give me some advice on praying?"

Good question.

I began by telling him a story that the author Brennan Manning tells. He had been asked to visit an elderly man and when he arrived, the man was in bed surrounded by lots of books. "Tell me, Brennan," he asked, "What is prayer? I have read all these theological books, but I still don't get it."

Brennan pointed to an empty chair next to the bed and said, "See that empty chair. I want you to imagine that Jesus is sitting there. All you have to do is simply start talking with him."

The old man was amazed, "Is that it? I really get that." He went on, "When you are gone, I'm going to have a conversation with Jesus!"

Six months' later, Brennan saw the old man's daughter. "How is your father?" he asked.

"He died about a month ago," she replied. "And here's the strange thing. When I discovered him, he was not in bed but kneeling by a chair with his head on the seat."

"I'm so sorry for your loss," Brennan said, "but it's good to know that he died in the lap of Jesus."

The woman looked very confused and so Brennan told her about the last conversation he'd had with her father.

Prayer is, first of all, a conversation with Jesus.

Prayer tips

- Go to your cell.

- Make yourself comfortable.

- Be still.

  The psalmist says, "I have calmed and quieted myself" (Psalm 131:2). This can be a hard thing to do as our minds are filled with a thousand and one things. But take some time just to be quiet.

- Ask the Lord to come and fill you with the Holy Spirit.

- God loves you. Meditate on that for a few minutes. Let its truth stir your soul and settle in your mind.

- Thank God that He loves you. If you find that a difficult concept, ask God to begin the process of healing your heart.

  Thank God for the small things that you have noticed; thank Him for the great things. And if you can't find anything to thank Him for, simply find a 'thank you' Psalm and slowly read it aloud.

- Read from the Bible.

    There are many good books and apps on Bible reflections. Find yourself one. Turn to the appropriate date and read the short passage.

    Is God speaking to you through it? If so, write it down.

- Look ahead to the day/tomorrow and commit whatever is planned to God. Pray for the people you are going to meet.

- Pray for others. I have a list of people I pray for, some daily, others weekly (the list is getting longer!). Once a week I pray for the council and government. Lift the name of each person to God and pray the Lord's blessing on them.

- Talk to Him as a best friend.

- Tell Him you are sorry for anything that may have hurt Him and others. Talk to Him about what is on your heart: joy, pain, hopes and disappointments.

- Simply be real and honest.

- Allow space for some silence – to hear the whispers of His Spirit.

- Leave with a thankful heart.

A daily spiritual practice that can be done in three minutes!

Last thing at night as I lie down and close my eyes, I simply look back over the day.

I start from when I first woke up, go through the day and remember who I have met. I thank God for them and ask His blessing on them.

In this process, I check my heart and if there is anything I need to put right I do it! I ask for God's forgiveness.

Finally, I thank God for my wife, Jane.

And then I go to sleep.

Go on! We all can do this.

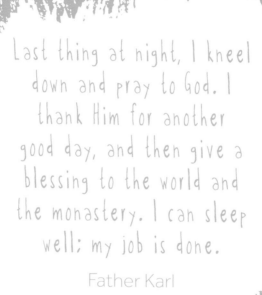

Last thing at night, I kneel down and pray to God. I thank Him for another good day, and then give a blessing to the world and the monastery. I can sleep well; my job is done.

Father Karl

Keeping a journal

In the Old Testament, there are stories of how at significant moments when God moved or spoke, the Israelites would erect something called *massebahs*. This is a Hebrew word and means 'standing stone' – perhaps think of the type of stones at Stonehenge.

The Israelites did this to mark and record the place that God had spoken and acted. A principal reason for this was so that later on they could return to the spot and remind themselves what He really had done and said. Many years may have passed, but every time they saw that standing stone, they would remember.

A part of my spiritual rhythm that I have found very helpful is keeping a journal.

Over the years, I have kept a journal and it stays in my cell. In it I date the entries and record verses, prayers, thankfulness and things I feel God has spoken to me. I find it so helpful – especially looking back and seeing the hand of God on my life.

It records major events in my life, and it's a place where I sometimes write my prayers.

To help me with my prayers I have photographs, notes, stones, paintings. Most of these are visual and remind me of a specific need.

Cardiff, the city I love and pray for.

This pebble on my desk reminds me of the specific moment when I made a commitment to God about something.

Paul
John
Liz

People I pray for on a daily and weekly basis.

Don't enjoy reading or writing?

As I've said before, people learn in many different ways. If you enjoy words, the thought of keeping a written journal as part of your spiritual practice will be exciting!

However, if you're dyslexic, or really struggle with writing, the idea of keeping a written journal ... well, it's not going to happen.

But there are other ways to keep journals.

- Most of us have phones that record. You could use it to audio-record all that you learn in the cell. You can create separate chapters for each day.

- You could start a video blog. Visuals help me to remember. For example, I have a photograph of a painting that God used to speak to me. Every time I see it, I am reminded of what God said to me.

- Take photos of images through which God has spoken to you.

- Paint or sketch. I sometimes paint or sketch prayers that words can't express. They are a clear marker to me that God spoke to me.

However you do it, I would encourage you to make a start.

Create your own *massebah*.

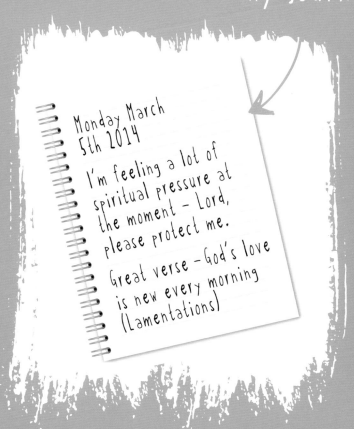

Monday March
5th 2014

I'm feeling a lot of
spiritual pressure at
the moment — Lord,
please protect me.

Great verse — God's love
is new every morning
(Lamentations)

Journaling – don't know where to start?

Reflect on the last 24 hours, then write the answers to these questions in your journal.

- What are you thankful for?

- What caused you pain?

- Where did you sense the presence of God?

- Where did you feel the lack of His presence?

Ready to listen

4

Owning our story can be hard but not nearly as difficult as spending our lives running from it. Embracing our vulnerabilities is risky but not nearly as dangerous as giving up on love and belonging and joy — the experiences that make us the most vulnerable.

Brené Brown

Vulnerability

Jane and I were on holiday, and as usual we took some books with us. For me, these ranged from an Ian Rankin thriller, a book called *Anatomy of the Soul* by Dr Curt Thompson and a great book by Brené Brown, *Daring Greatly*. Jane had a copy of *Sacred Space: The Prayer Book* by the Irish Jesuits.

As I read, two of the books referred to the story of how Peter was asked three times by Jesus, "Do you love me?" and three times Peter replied, "Yes". At the same time, Jane read me a section from *Sacred Space* that focused on Jesus saying to His disciples that He no longer called them servants but friends. The comment that went with this was, "Faith is an affair of the heart."

Something inside me reacted; something in my gut told me that all was not right with my soul.

Then Jane then asked me a question. "Do you love God, Paul?" Instantly, I replied, "Of course." Then came the killer question:

"Are you falling in love with God?"

There it was.

It was out.

My soul was shouting "No!"

I was a follower of Jesus. And I believed in God. But did I really *love* Him?

In *Anatomy of the Soul*, Curt Thompson makes the point that the brain is divided into two. One side is primarily interested in information – books, talks, the more of the stuff the better! The other side of the brain is to do with our emotions, feelings and creativity.

For hundreds of years the Western church has focused on the information side. So Bible readings, commentaries, books, didactic talks and so on, are what we feed on.

There is absolutely nothing wrong with this, and I would encourage all of us to be engaged in all of those things.

However, the West has been very poor at nurturing the emotional, creative side and has generally ignored it. But if the statement "Faith is an affair of the heart" is true, the result is that one day we will wake up and discover that our faith is cold.

We have all the head knowledge about God, but there is no emotional engagement.

Nothing is more practical than finding God, that is, than falling in love in a quite absolute, final way. What you are in love with, what seizes your imagination, will affect everything. It will decide what will get you out of bed in the morning, what you will do with your evenings, how you spend your weekends, what you read, whom you know, what breaks your heart, and amazes you with joy and gratitude. Fall in love, stay in love, and it will decide everything.

Pedro Arrupe

Soul care is about both sides of the brain and vulnerability is an essential part of it because it opens up that side of the brain that is neglected.

The word vulnerability comes from the Latin *vulnerare* and means 'to wound', 'to be capable of being wounded'.

Brené Brown defines vulnerability as "uncertainty, risk, and emotional exposure."

When you are vulnerable, you are intentionally opening up a side of your life that is normally hidden to others.

And that creates the possibility of being hurt.

A few years ago, I took up painting. I found it very enjoyable and an outlet for my creativity. But nobody, apart from Jane, saw my paintings. And then an art gallery I was involved with asked me to put one on display in an exhibition from local artists. For some unknown reason I said yes!

To say I got more nervous as the exhibition approached would be a huge understatement.

And on the day of the official opening, I was scared.

Very scared!

It's not about perfection.
It's not about adequacy.
It's not about your competence ...
It's about holding on to God,
because the soul was made to be
connected with Him.

John Ortberg

Why? It's simple really: other people would see my painting and have opinions, which could well be ... negative! Having made myself vulnerable, there was a great danger that I would interpret their opinion of the painting as a comment on my value as a human being!

For some of us, the risk of negative comments and the fear of rejection means we close the door on vulnerability.

That is a great pity, as one of the keys to a healthy soul is vulnerability.

To take a risk.

To step out in faith.

To share some of what is going on inside me.

If we close the door on vulnerability, then we run the risk that our heart will grow cold.

We need to be vulnerable.

We need friends who we can be vulnerable with.

We need good friends that we can simply pour out our heart and questions to.

Who do you have in your life that you can be completely open with? They would be people with whom you could share failings, fears and questions such as:

"I struggle with pornography."
"I have bouts of anxiety."
"I'm really struggling to pray."
"My marriage is going through a difficult time."
"I'm scared."
"I'm having doubts about the faith."

If we are to live how God intended, we need to be vulnerable and our role model in that is Jesus.

Life is forged in the
difficult places

"Think of yourselves the way Christ Jesus thought of Himself. He had equal status with God but didn't think so much of himself that He had to cling to the advantages of that status no matter what. Not at all. When the time came, He set aside the privileges of deity and took on the status of a slave, became human! Having become human, He stayed human. It was an incredibly humbling process. He didn't claim special privileges. Instead, He lived a selfless, obedient life and then died a selfless, obedient death – and the worst kind of death at that – a crucifixion" (Philippians 2:5–8, The Message).

This is the Son of God who took on flesh and bone and was born as a baby, totally and completely dependent on His parents.

We follow a God who made Himself utterly vulnerable.

Let's do the same!

Vulnerability is the birthplace of love, belonging, joy, courage, empathy, and creativity. It is the source of hope, empathy, accountability, and authenticity. If we want greater clarity in our purpose or deeper and more meaningful spiritual lives, vulnerability is the path.

Brené Brown

Connecting – friends matter

I'd just had a difficult meeting and was feeling very low. It had not gone in the direction that I'd anticipated, so I was very disappointed. Worse, however, was a very personal comment that someone in the meeting had made to me in front of all the others.

I felt hurt and angry and went home knowing that this would keep me awake. And sure enough, I slept fitfully and in the waking times I was arguing my case with the person who'd made the comment (I always won!).

However, in the light of the morning I still felt bad. So I called my best friend and we met for a coffee. I did what I always do in these situations and just off-loaded all that I was feeling. My friend simply listened. And to top it all, I then burst into tears – in the coffee shop!

I talked and then listened to my friend. Over the next hour or so I began to see the meeting in a different light, and I got to the place where I could go to see the person who had upset me and talk it through.

Without friends like the one who met up with me in the coffee shop, I would not survive. I need their support.

Who are your closest friends? Those who are there for you at all times, through bad and good? The friends who lift you when you are down and challenge you when you need it?

These people are the cornerstone of our lives.

Without them we would not survive.

Sociologists and psychologists tell us that because of the amount of time given in relationships like these, we can't sustain more than an average of five or six close friendships. I think it's great if we have two!

It should be no surprise that we need one another.

In the Celtic tradition, they celebrate the Trinity joyfully, describing it as a dance of Father, Son and Holy Sprit.

The Trinity has also been described as a community.

Three in one and one in three – all dependent on one another.

We are made in the image of God. God is plural – Father, Son and Holy Spirit. We are created for community. Part of our DNA is to be there for one another.

An intrinsic part of soul care is having friends who know the best and worst about us but are still there!

Making friendship work

Give your time

Relationships need time. We can't develop a supportive relationship in just five minutes.

We and our friend need to be able to have complete trust that confidentiality will be maintained.

We need to meet regularly – perhaps once a month, but also be available to each other at any time that one of us is in a crisis.

Be teachable

Do we want to grow as a person? Do we want to be someone who is willing to change? If so, we need a teachable spirit.

When people share critical insights into something we have done or said, do we immediately become defensive or do we try to listen with objective ears? When your friend tells you some hard truths, do you accept it or do you try and defend yourself?

Be sacrificial

Friendships work both ways. Our friends are there for us at any time, which means that we need to be there for them at any time!

Friendship means we will sacrifice our time and energy to help our friends. It means we are prepared to drop something if they call and ask for help. This is a sacrifice.

Listen

Good friends listen well.

Dr Jerome Groopman at Harvard Medical School observed that, on average, a doctor interrupts his patients 18 seconds after they have started. All I can say is that I'm thankful that's not the case with my doctor. Mine is a very good listener.

Most of us don't listen well. Most of us want to share our opinions and views. A good friend is one who will listen and reflect on what is being said. Be a good friend and listen!

Every day we take 26,000 breaths.
That's 14,000 litres of air.

We should breathe from our stomach,
not our chest. When stressed, most of
us breathe through our chest.

Without breath, we die.

Without soul care, we die.

Learning the language of God

We've already touched on one of the hardest aspects of soul care, which is simply making space to listen to God. But what if we realised that God wants to speak to us all the time – wherever we may be?

The Lord is more determined and excited to speak to us than we are to hear from Him. We must realise that God is always speaking, but He is not human and His first language is not English! Once we understand the diverse ways in which He does speak, we begin to appreciate that maybe God speaks to us more than we realise.

Over the next few pages I will share some of the ways in which He does this.

Scripture

God speaks to us through scripture. He brings it alive to us by His Spirit, and through it provides a way for us to check revelation. Often He will highlight a verse or a story that speaks to us about our circumstances.

God's still small voice

At times God speaks to us in a still small voice from within our spirit. This can be heard as a passing thought, sudden impression, or internal sense of something God is saying. This still small voice is illustrated in 1 Kings. In this account, God is not in the strong wind or the earthquake; He is in the gentle whisper:

"The Lord said, 'Go out and stand on the mountain in the presence of the Lord, for the Lord is about to pass by.'

"Then a great and powerful wind tore the mountains apart and shattered the rocks before the Lord, but the Lord was not in the wind. After the wind there was an earthquake, but the Lord was not in the earthquake. After the earthquake came a fire, but the Lord was not in the fire. And after the fire came a gentle whisper. When Elijah heard it, he pulled his cloak over his face and went out and stood at the mouth of the cave.

"Then a voice said to him, 'What are you doing here, Elijah?'" (1 Kings 19:11–13).

We need to hear the still small voice.

Creation

Creation itself is a voice from the Lord and speaks to us in many ways. The obvious way is that God's creation tells us about who He is. The mountains speak of His strength, the rivers His provision, and the flowers His beauty.

Creation also worships:

"Let the heavens rejoice, let the earth be glad; let the sea resound, and all that is in it. Let the fields be jubilant, and everything in them; let all the trees of the forest sing for joy" (Psalm 96:11–12).

Simply by walking in and through nature we are refreshed, emotionally, spiritually and physically.

Visions and dreams

A common way the Lord communicates with us is through visions and dreams.

Visions

There are two types of visions. The first one is a vision of the mind in which the Lord 'projects' images and pictures onto the 'screen' of our minds.

This can be called prophetic imagination or imagination that is under the influence of the Holy Spirit.

The second type of vision is an open vision. This is an image that you see with your natural eyes.

Dreams

Not all dreams are from God, but they can be a place where God speaks to His people. Many people in the Bible had dreams where this happened.

Prophetic acts

Often the Lord will direct someone to do a prophetic act. This was common in the Bible; for example, Jeremiah set a brick in the middle of the city as a prophetic symbol of a siege wall being laid against Israel, and Agabus tied a belt around himself as a way of showing Paul how he would suffer.

Coming over to us, he took Paul's belt, tied his own hands and feet with it and said, "The Holy Spirit says, 'In this way the Jews of Jerusalem will bind the owner of this belt and will hand him over to the Gentiles'" (Acts 21:11).

Prophetic words

In the Bible it talks about the gift of prophecy (Romans 12:6 and 1 Corinthians 12:10). This is where the Lord speaks through one person to another by giving them a message, impression or a picture. A prophetic word is always strengthening, encouraging and comforting.

Circumstances

God can speak to us and direct us through the circumstances of our lives. This dynamic often occurs as God opens and closes the doors of opportunity.

It is easy to misunderstand this principle and account everything that happens in our life to God, but we need to practise discernment. Recognising that God can be speaking through our circumstances is helpful in growing in the language of God.

Junk

Everything can be taken
from a man but one thing:
the last of the human
freedoms – to choose one's
attitude in any given set
of circumstances.

Victor E. Frankl

Making the journey easier

There are some things we need to accept about our lives and the sooner we do this the easier our journey will be.

For example, I learned very early on not to take myself too seriously!

This one realisation has made my journey through life much easier.

These are a few more things I accepted about myself:

- I don't have all the answers.
- The church and Christianity will survive very well without me.
- Life does not revolve around me.
- I'm not the next best answer to … (fill in the blank!)
- I will die one day.

No matter what our:

    background
    home life
    school
    friends
    work
    status

we each carry baggage and we are all damaged in some way.

For the fortunate some, the damage and the baggage is light. For many others, it is not.

As part of our spiritual rhythm, we need to learn how to deal with our baggage.

At the start of the book I wrote about what it is to be human: we are fearfully and wonderfully made, but with a serious flaw!

Most people believe the second part of that sentence more than the first. I think I can safely say that most of us do not live in the reality of the first part.

To continue the journey into living in the reality of "I am fearfully and wonderfully made but with a serious flaw" and, furthermore, live with the reality that God loves us, we need to deal with some of the lies and rubbish that have cluttered our lives:

- Words that hurt
- Others' actions
- Bad decisions
- Regrets
- Bitterness
- Envy

Lies we
tell ourselves

I am a mistake.

I am a burden.

I am stupid.

I am worthless.

I am not allowed to make mistakes.

I must be approved by certain people to feel OK.

I don't have the right to experience joy and pleasure.

I don't have the right to assert myself
and say what I think and feel.

I don't have a right to feel.

I am valued for my intelligence, wealth,
and what I do; not for who I am.

Why carry so much
emotional rubbish in your life?

Bin it!

Four of the most powerful sentences you could ever say:

- I love you.
- I am sorry!
- Please forgive me.
- I forgive you!

Go on, say them – even if it's to yourself.

A new world awaits you.

Forgiveness

If someone has said something that has hurt you, forgive them. (Of course, that's a lot easier said than done, and we may often have to go through a long and painful journey before, with God's help, we are able to do that).

If you are able to, and it's appropriate, go and talk to the person and explain how their comments or actions had upset you but that you have forgiven them.

If you are not at the place to do this, or you don't feel it's appropriate, go and talk it through with someone you trust.

All of us have disappointments and failures.

Bin them!

Let them go!

Don't spend your time with regret.

Imagine, instead, all that can be done with God ... and go for it.

Be generous. You can't lose!

Forgiveness
is not
an occasional act;
it is a
constant attitude.

Martin Luther King, Jr

Above all else,
guard your heart,
for everything you do
flows from it.

Proverbs 4:23

Best practice

6

Develop a
thankful
heart

Hating that treadmill!

It's a cold and wet morning, and I'm driving to a place I both love and hate – the sports club. I try to go three or four times a week because I realise that while it takes a lot of effort, the benefit is great. I go at a time that works for me and I do about 40 minutes of different exercises.

Doctors tell us that when we exercise it releases endorphins into our brain. These contribute to a feeling of well-being.

And we all want a feeling of well-being – whatever it is!

I have also discovered that when I exercise it helps with stress.

It makes me feel more alive.

It helps me cope better.

Most of us do not get excited about exercising.

So create a routine that works for you.

You don't have to go to the gym to exercise, you can just add things into your day that are achievable.

Here are some suggestions:

- Go for a walk – 30 minutes a day, four days a week.
- When shopping, walk up the stairs – don't take the lift.
- Cycle for 30 minutes a day.
- Swim in your local leisure centre.
- Play tennis.
- Join a local ramblers' club.

Go on, give it a go and make it part of your daily rhythm.

The gathered community

As I write, the church in the West is at a crossroads. The last 20 years has seen a real disillusionment with 'traditional' church. Some people, rightly, have begun to ask, what is church meant to be?

Some embarked on deconstructing church and building it back up again. Others have come to the conclusion that the church is no longer important, in particular the Sunday gathering.

Some have given up on church.

Some say it is no longer needed.

Some say you don't need large gatherings; church can be two or three people coming together.

Two words have dominated the discussion: 'emergent' and 'emerging', reflecting a radical redesign of church. The issue, it is argued, is to do with separating the form and function of the church. The function should be timeless, but the form should always be changing and evolving.

As such, we have seen the birth of churches that meet in pubs and coffee shops; there have been churches built around surfing communities!

These are wonderful developments that reveal the evolving nature and form of church. But the critical thing we need to hold on to is this: it's the *form* that church takes that changes, not its *function*.

Whatever expression of church we believe in, it is essential that we realise that the gathered community, which largely expresses itself on a Sunday morning (although can be on other days), is vital to our well-being and a non-negotiable part of soul care.

I know that when the church is bad, it is a disaster. Through a bad expression of church many people have been hurt, wounded, damaged, and broken.

And I am truly sorry when those experiences happen, because it's not the way it's meant to be.

But don't give up on church.

We need each other!

Church is far more than a Sunday gathering. Church is 24 hours a day and seven days a week.

However, the Sunday gathering is an essential part of it. A spiritual dynamic goes on that we experience nowhere else.

I love this church, this living, pulsating, sinning people of
God with a crucifying passion. Why?

For all the Christian hate, I experience here a community of love.

For all the institutional madness, I find here a tradition of reason.

For all the individual repression, I breathe here an air of freedom.

For all the fear of sex, I discover here the redemption of my body.

In an age so inhuman, I touch here tears of compassion.

In a world so grim and humourless, I share here rich joy
and earthly laughter.

In the midst of death, I hear an incomparable stress on life.

For all the apparent absence of God, I sense here the
real presence of Jesus.

Walter Burghardt

It is an essential part of our soul care, and by not committing to church we rob ourselves, and the people who are there, of something precious.

Local church is where I gather with people from a large range of life. In this context, I serve God and share His love. In this context, I learn as I serve alongside people who are different from me. In this safe space, God speaks to me and brings healing through His body.

Church is God's idea. It is His plan.

There is no plan B.

If you want to get a sense of the heart of God about church, just take a look at the wonderful image that He uses to describe it.

He calls the church Jesus' bride.

I have participated at many weddings as a church leader, and I have stood at the front as a husband-to-be, and one thing I know for certain is that the bride always looks stunning!

I want the church, the bride of Jesus, to be stunning when He comes to claim her. If you are not already part of a local church, go and find one!

Authentic spirituality
speaks to God
with sincerity
and helps us
become more like Jesus.

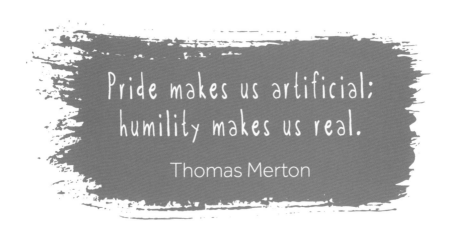

Pride makes us artificial;
humility makes us real.

Thomas Merton

Encouragement

I was in church the other day when one of our older ladies, Val, walked in. I had just discovered that it was her 82nd birthday. And as soon as I saw her, I said, "Happy birthday!"

To my surprise, her face lit up. I wasn't surprised that she smiled, but rather that her reaction seemed to be disproportionate to the very small thing I had just said to her.

But it mattered to her because these few words of mine told her that she was known, loved, and valued.

It was a very simple thing to wish someone a happy birthday, but it made her day!

My wife is an encourager; it is one of her gifts. She writes hundreds of cards every year to people to celebrate birthdays, engagements, births, new jobs – the list is almost endless.

She also writes cards to people who are struggling, dealing with loss, and facing tough choices. And she writes cards when she feels the prompting of the Holy Spirit.

The effect of receiving these cards is huge. People feel affirmed, encouraged, and of value.

It's a great thing to do.

So here's a couple of questions:

When you meet up with your friends, family, neighbours, and colleagues, are they lifted by your presence or do they feel weary from it?

When they leave you, do they walk away with a sense of well-being, or are they just glad that they have got away because you're hard work?

Why do I, and so many of us, struggle with this concept of encouragement?

Why do we so often find it easier to say negative things rather than positive comments?

It's probably because most of us don't have the gift of encouragement, but here's something important to take in: we can *learn* how to do it.

The next time you meet someone, do or say something that is encouraging.

Or better still, be proactive and:

- Send someone a text today with a word of encouragement.
- Send a card to a friend.
- Buy someone a coffee and listen to them.
- Offer to help someone.

If we do this, it's not only good for them, but it's good for our soul because I've found that when I encourage people not only does it bless them, but the process also blesses me!

God loves you.
But I'm His favourite!

Laughter

Does laughter have anything to do with soul care?

The answer is a resounding yes!

Laughter is a wonderful gift that God has given us. The quote on the opposite page is taken from a card I bought in a shop. When I saw it, it simply made me chuckle.

Recently I spoke at a conference on the theme of soul care. At the end, the participants were asked to share anything encouraging that they'd take away from what I'd said.

Some of the answers they might have given were:

"Great Bible teacher!"

"Discerning insights!"

"Excellent leader!"

I could have lived off any of those.

However, no one said that. In fact, the vast majority said the same thing:

"Paul allowed us to laugh."

I know what you're thinking – there couldn't have been too much to what I shared. In fact, if we are honest, the feedback made me seem a bit shallow.

But I went home very happy.

Laughter is a great healer. Laughter helps sooth an aching soul.

So learn to laugh. Not at people, but *with* them.

A happy heart
makes the
face cheerful.

Proverbs 15:13

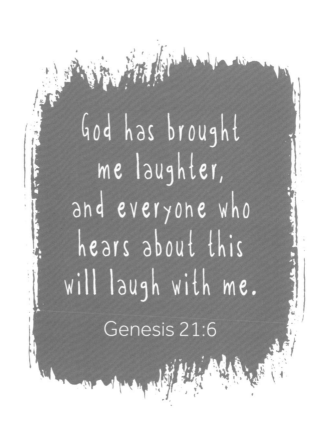

God has brought
me laughter,
and everyone who
hears about this
will laugh with me.

Genesis 21:6

Learning from other traditions

One thing that I have discovered over the years is that there is an incredibly rich and varied spiritual heritage to our faith. There are so many differences between Christian traditions, and yet they all share many common values:

- A love of Jesus.

- A desire to know more of God.

- A love of the scriptures.

- A desire to bless others.

But they also have distinctives and this is often reflected in their spiritual practices.

Over the next few pages, I will share some of these, and if there are any helpful practices with which you are unfamiliar, you might like to try to incorporate them in your own daily rhythm.

I hope they will be of help.

I think the most important
thing that happens
within Christian spirituality
is when the person falls in love
with Jesus.

Donald Miller

Rhythms of life from Small Boat Big Sea

This is a community in Australia that have committed themselves to live out the four values below. They meet weekly and ask themselves these questions:

Blessing
Who have you blessed this week through words or actions, and what learning, encouragement or concerns were raised by it?

Eating
With whom have you eaten this week, and what learning, encouragement or concerns were raised by it?

Listening
Have you heard or sensed any promptings from God this week?

What passages of scripture have encouraged you or what other resources have enriched your growth as a Christian this week?

Sentness
In what ways have you sensed yourself carrying on the work of God in your daily life this week?

Be joyful.
Do the little things.
Keep the faith.

St David, the patron saint of Wales

Rhythms of life from the Iona Community

Have a soul friend you meet with at least six times a year.

Share with this soul friend how God has led you since the last time you met and what God has been saying to you about the future.

Go on a retreat once every six months and if possible, spend a whole day. Find a place of solitude and silence.

Visit a 'thin place'. This is a place where the gap between heaven and earth seems so thin, and there is a real, tangible presence of God.

Make space for a daily time of prayer. This can be as little as five minutes a day.

Keep a journal of your thoughts, lessons and things you sense God is saying.

Rhythms of life from St Ignatius of Loyola

Reserve some space on a weekly basis in a place where you will not be disturbed or distracted.

Reflect on a moment in your day or week when you felt most grateful – the moment you felt most alive. When were you most able to give and receive love in this situation?

Reflect on a moment in your day or week when you felt least grateful, when you were least able to give and receive love, when you felt angry, drained and lifeless. Be honest with yourself. What could this situation reveal to you about God and His love for you?

Finally, do not form any judgements about yourself and others, but simply give thanks for both situations, and seek God's love to support and sustain you just as you are.

After a time of silent prayer, seeking to receive from God, write down your thoughts and prayers.

Last thoughts

(but still very important)

In solitude I get rid of
my scaffolding:
no friends to talk with,
no phone calls to make,
no books to distract,
just me, naked, vulnerable,
weak, sinful, deprived, broken
– nothing.

Henri Nouwen

The spiritual security of insecurity

I recently came across a wonderful phrase that I believe explains a state that many followers of Jesus live in:

'cognitive dissonance'.

- Cognition – the mental process of acquiring knowledge and understanding through our thoughts, experience and the senses – i.e how our mind works.

- Dissonance – discord, conflict.

Simply put, many of us are living our lives in conflict with what we believe and think.

What it means is that we are simultaneously holding two or more contradictory beliefs, ideas and values.

Perhaps our long-held views have suddenly been challenged by something persuasive that is diametrically opposed to them.

If the clash remains unresolved, we suffer mental discomfort (psychological stress).

For example, we know smoking is bad for us and that in all probability it will shorten our life, but despite this we keep on smoking. That is cognitive dissonance.

In this particular example, how to we resolve this? There are three options:

1. Stop smoking – the best solution!
2. Convince yourself that the research into smoking is wrong.
3. Justify smoking with a number of reasons, such as that it helps to calm you, etc.

Choosing options 2 or 3 will leave you in a place of cognitive dissonance, a place of tension.

People of faith sometimes experience this cognitive dissonance.

Take John the Baptist, who is described by Jesus as one of the greatest men who ever lived. John was one of the first to recognise that Jesus was the Messiah. John had a world view that saw the Messiah as a liberator who would lead a rebellion against the occupying force – Rome.

He believed that Jesus was the Messiah and became His follower. Jesus would deliver them. All would be well.

But then John was arrested and locked up in prison.

This was not part of the plan.

Following Jesus was meant to be about victory, not defeat. All of a sudden, John experiences cognitive dissonance: his strongly held beliefs are challenged by his circumstances. So he sends a message to Jesus:

"Are you really the Messiah?"

He needed an answer.

Jesus does not even go to visit him!

Instead, He tells one of his disciples to go to John and report what is happening:

"The blind receive sight, the lame walk, those who have leprosy are cleansed, the deaf hear, the dead are raised up, and the good news is proclaimed to the poor" (Matthew 11:5).

In other words, "John, your world view needs to change."

I have noticed a pattern develop among a group of people who grew up in a faith culture of the 60s and 70s. Faith was defined by certainty in what they believed and was black and white on a number of issues.

However, when these people hit a certain age – usually over 50 – some of the arguments for their 'certainties' seem to crumble. Some of their firmly held beliefs have been challenged, and it leads them to a place of confusion about the rest of their faith.

At this point they face two obstacles – in effect what we may call a perfect storm.

- Their framework of belief begins to crumble.
- The West's fascination with information and knowledge has underpinned their lives to the detriment of their emotional and creative side.

And this has resulted in a heart connection to God that is cold.

One of the goals of this book is to help us develop our emotional and spiritual well-being: to help us keep our heart in touch with God.

But I also believe that for the information side of the brain, there is a model that could help us deal with the challenges of uncertainty.

Part of the answer lies in recognising that there is often more than one place in which we can sit with regard to the questions of faith that challenge us.

There is no right or wrong place to be in and we will move from one to the other and back again. In fact, we will do this many times.

However, I have found it can really help our faith journey if we know where we sit at any given time.

Where do you best sit?

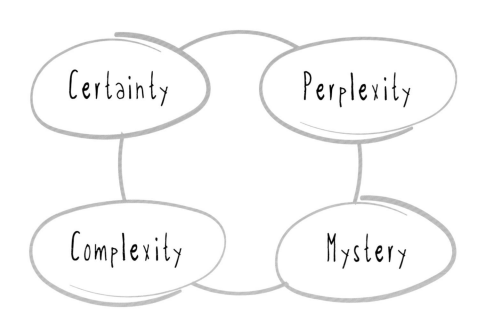

I attended a talk a few years ago in which the speaker helpfully suggested that there are four Christian worldviews which we can hold.

Certainty

This is a worldview that has strong, firmly held opinions about theological issues and does not allow for the possibility of other interpretations or opposing views. The questions of life and faith have black and white answers, so in this circle there is no room for 'grey zones' where uncertainties lie.

Complexity

Sees that faith is not straightforward. For example, this could include the fact that science appears to bring a counter-argument to seven-day creationism.

Perplexity

Faith seems very confusing sometimes. You have a friend with cancer. You spend months in intensive prayer, calling the church to periods of fasting. Yet your friend still dies. You watch news of all the suffering around the world.

Believing in a loving God in these situations is challenging and perplexing.

Mystery

An acknowledgement that there are many questions and fewer answers. This is the place that Job arrives in at the end of his discussions with God. We recognise that life is a mystery, but at the heart of it is a God of love.

This love is manifested in His Son, Jesus.

Being in a place of mystery means: "I trust Jesus for all I don't understand."

I have learned that in our Christian life, all of us sit in one of these circles and we constantly move from one to another. It is not a linear journey, where we move from one place to the next one and end up in the final destination – mystery. Rather, they are all connected by a circle and we move around it, backwards and forwards. The most important principle in *Soul Care* is to recognise that each circle is a legitimate place in which to sit.

However, when we have questions, doubts and crises of faith, then I believe that we need to be sitting in a place of mystery, simply loving and trusting Jesus.

"I'm convinced: You can do anything and everything.
Nothing and no one can upset your plans. You asked,
'Who is this muddying the water, ignorantly confusing
the issue, second-guessing my purposes?' I admit it.
I was the one. I babbled on about things far beyond me,
made small talk about wonders way over my head.
You told me, 'Listen, and let me do the talking. Let me
ask the questions. You give the answers.'"

Job 42:1–4, The Message

And finally, my very best bit of advice?

Keep loving Jesus.

May the Lord bless you and keep you;
may the Lord make His face shine on you
and be gracious to you.

May the Lord lift up His countenance
before you, and give you His peace.

Numbers 6: 24–26